Enslow PUBLISHING

BY KATHRYN WALTON

VOL. I FROM PAST TO PRESIDENT 1797

JOHN ADAMS

Please visit our website, www.enslow.com. For a free color catalog of all our high-quality books, call toll free 1-800-398-2504 or fax 1-877-980-4454.

Library of Congress Cataloging-in-Publication Data

Names: Walton, Kathryn, 1993- author.
Title: John Adams / Kathryn Walton.
Description: Buffalo, NY : Enslow Publishing, [2025] | Series: From past to president | Includes index.
Identifiers: LCCN 2024034395 (print) | LCCN 2024034396 (ebook) | ISBN 9781978542433 (library binding) | ISBN 9781978542426 (paperback) | ISBN 9781978542440 (ebook)
Subjects: LCSH: Adams, John, 1735-1826–Juvenile literature. | Lawyers–United States–Biography–Juvenile literature. | Presidents–United States–Biography–Juvenile literature.
Classification: LCC E322 .W35 2025 (print) | LCC E322 (ebook) | DDC 973.4/4/092 [B]–dc23/eng/20240801
LC record available at https://lccn.loc.gov/2024034395
LC ebook record available at https://lccn.loc.gov/2024034396

Published in 2025 by
Enslow Publishing
2544 Clinton Street
Buffalo, NY 14224

Copyright © 2025 Enslow Publishing

Portions of this work were originally authored by M. H. Seeley and published as *Before John Adams Was President*. All new material in this edition is authored by Kathryn Walton.

Designer: Claire Zimmermann
Editor: Natalie Humphrey

Photo credits: Cover (John Adams portrait, signature), pp. 11, 13 (left), 15 courtesy of the Library of Congress; cover (Harvard University engraving), p. 6 Morphart Creation/Shutterstock.com; cover (newspaper clipping) STILLFX/Shutterstock.com; cover (image at top left) Prachaya Roekdeethaweesab/Shutterstock.com; cover, p. 7 (home) Faina Gurevich/Shutterstock.com; cover (author name scrap), series art (caption background) Robyn Mackenzie/Shutterstock.com; series art (red paper background) OLeksiiTooz/Shutterstock.com; cover (newspaper text background at lower left) MaryValery/Shutterstock.com; series art (newspaper text background) TanyaFox/Shutterstock.com; series art (More to Learn antique tag) Mega Pixel/
Shutterstock.com; pp. 5, 7, 9, 13, 15, 19 (ripped blank newspaper piece) STILLFX/Shutterstock.com; pp. 5, 9, 19 Everett Collection/Shutterstock.com; p. 13 (right) Charles_Willson_Peale_-_George_Washington_at_the_Battle_of_Princeton_-_Google_Art_Project.jpg/Wikimedia Commons; p. 17 299805/National Archives Catalog.

Some of the images in this book illustrate individuals who are models. The depictions do not imply actual situations or events.

All rights reserved. No part of this book may be reproduced in any form without permission in writing from the publisher, except by a reviewer.

Printed in the United States of America

CPSIA compliance information: Batch #CWENS25: For further information contact Enslow Publishing at 1-800-398-2504.

Find us on

CONTENTS

President John Adams 4

A Farmer's Life. 6

Abigail Adams 8

The Boston Massacre Trial 10

Choosing a Side. 12

Leading the Revolution 14

Ending the War. 16

Vice President Adams 18

Remembering President John Adams 20

President Adams's Timeline 21

Glossary 22

For More Information 23

Index 24

Words in the glossary appear in **bold** type the first time they are used in the text.

PRESIDENT
JOHN ADAMS

For much of his life, John Adams was well known as a great thinker. He was a U.S. president, but today he is remembered more for what he thought a president should be than his time in office. He wrote many **essays** about **democracy**, leadership, and **politics**. Many of these essays are still studied today!

John Adams was born on October 30, 1735, in Braintree, now known as Quincy, Massachusetts. His parents wanted him to become a minister, or a person who leads church services.

John Adams was the second president of the United States.

MORE TO KNOW

John Adams had two younger brothers, Peter and Elihu.

A FARMER'S LIFE

When John Adams was young, he didn't like going to school. He wanted to be a farmer, like his father. Adams's father worried that being a farmer would be a waste of his son's cleverness.

One day, Adams's father took him out into the fields and made him farm for a full day, thinking the hard work would change Adams's mind. But Adams surprised his father. He said he wanted to become a farmer still!

MORE TO KNOW

Adams's father would later send him to private school. Adams stuck with his education then and would attend Harvard College at the age of 15.

John Adams's home in Massachusetts is now part of a national historical park.

ABIGAIL ADAMS

Adams married his wife, Abigail Smith, in 1764. Abigail's mother was against their marriage, but Abigail and Adams got married anyway. Abigail was the person Adams went to when he needed advice. He trusted her opinion, or thoughts, over everyone else's.

MORE TO KNOW

Women of Adams's time weren't given the same education as men. But Abigail read many books and taught herself much of what she knew.

John and Abigail's love was so strong that they sent more than 1,100 letters to each other during their lives.

Abigail was very smart. She was a strong voice for women's rights. In one of her famous letters to Adams, she wrote, "Remember the ladies … do not put such unlimited power into the hands of the husbands."

THE BOSTON
MASSACRE TRIAL

Like many other presidents, Adams worked as a **lawyer**. He worked in Boston, Massachusetts. He had only one **client** in his first year and lost the case. But by 1770, Adams had become a very successful lawyer.

In perhaps his most well-known case, Adams defended British soldiers who were part of the Boston Massacre. Other Boston lawyers didn't want to defend these soldiers, but Adams agreed to do it. In the end, none of his clients were sent to jail.

MORE TO KNOW

Adams's first job was as a schoolteacher. He only taught for a short time.

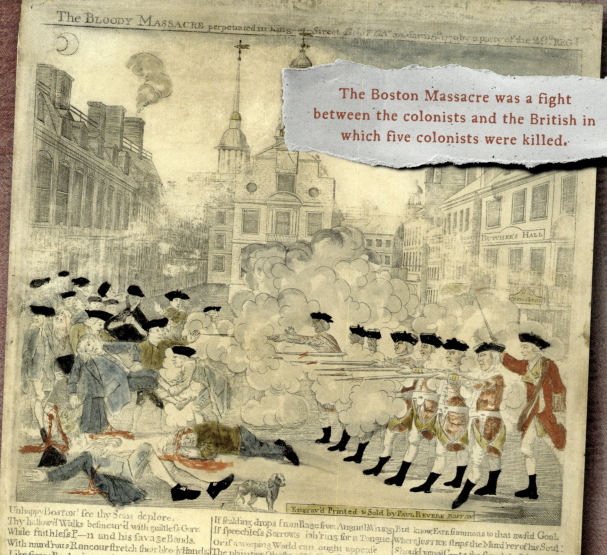

The Boston Massacre was a fight between the colonists and the British in which five colonists were killed.

CHOOSING A SIDE

In the late 1700s, many of the colonists were talking about breaking away from Great Britain. But Adams couldn't decide which side he was on! He didn't always like the way Britain ruled the colonies, but he also didn't trust everyone who spoke out in favor of American independence.

By the time the war began, Adams had made up his mind. The colonies needed to become an independent country to move forward.

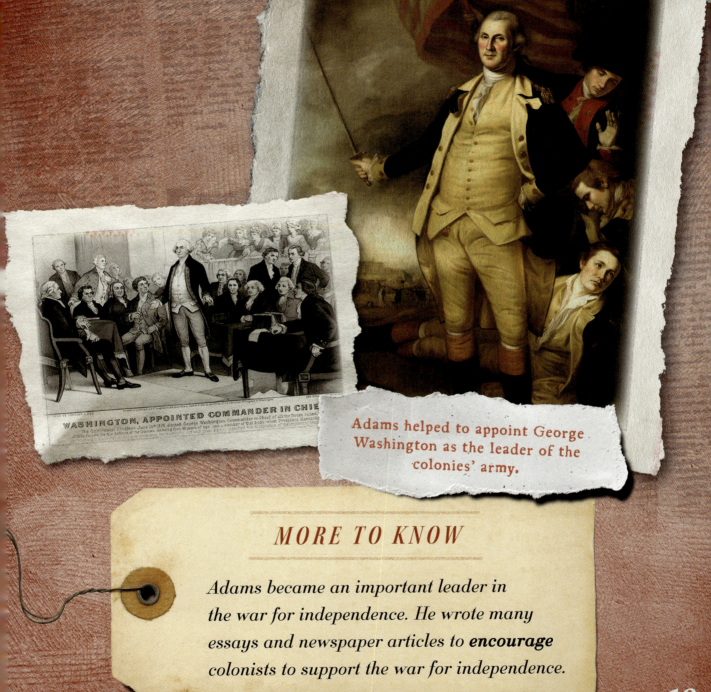

Adams helped to appoint George Washington as the leader of the colonies' army.

MORE TO KNOW

Adams became an important leader in the war for independence. He wrote many essays and newspaper articles to **encourage** colonists to support the war for independence.

13

LEADING
THE REVOLUTION

During the **American Revolution**, the Continental Congress was the governing body of the colonies. Adams joined the Continental Congress. He was chosen to help write the Declaration of Independence, the document that said the 13 American colonies were forming their own country.

Adams worked alongside some of the most respected men of his day, including Thomas Jefferson and Benjamin Franklin, to prepare the declaration. After it was written and agreed upon, 56 men from all 13 colonies signed it.

MORE TO KNOW

Only two people who signed the Declaration of Independence would later become president: Thomas Jefferson and John Adams!

The men chosen to write the Declaration of Independence were called the **Committee** of Five.

ENDING
THE WAR

Adams was a very busy man. He was part of 90 committees. This was more than any other member of the Congress! Adams was often sought out by leaders who wanted to know his thoughts.

In 1779, Adams was chosen to help the colonies come to an agreement for peace with Great Britain. He helped **negotiate** the Treaty of Paris, which ended the American Revolution. It also made Great Britain recognize the United States as its own country.

MORE TO KNOW

John Adams brought two of his sons, John Quincy and Charles, with him to Paris.

6.

the middle of said Communi...
Erie; through the midd...
until it arrives at the...
between that Lake &...
along the middle of sa...
nication into the La...
through the middle...
Water Communicat...
and Lake Superior...
Lake Superior Nor...
Royal & Philipeau...
Thence through...
Lake, and the...
between it & the...
said Lake of the...
the said Lake...
Point thereof...
due West Cou...
Thence by a...
the Middle...
until it...

15

without Difficulty and without requiring any Compensation.

Article 10th..

The solemn Ratifications of the present Treaty expedited in good & due Form shall be exchanged between the contracting Parties in the Space of Six Months or sooner if possible to be computed from the Day of the Signature of the present Treaty. In Witness whereof we the undersigned their Ministers Plenipotentiary have in their Name and in Virtue of our Full Powers signed with our Hands the present Definitive Treaty, and caused the Seals of our Arms to be affix'd thereto.

DONE at Paris, this third Day of September, In the Year of our Lord one thousand seven hundred & eighty three. —

D Hartley   John Adams.   B. Franklin   John Jay

The Treaty of Paris was signed in 1783.

VICE PRESIDENT
ADAMS

Adams believed no one person or group could rule a whole country. However, Adams also believed that for the country to succeed, it needed a strong leader. In 1789, Adams ran to become the first president of the United States. He lost to George Washington, but came in second place. At the time, that meant he would become the vice president.

Adams was unhappy with his role. He believed the office of the vice president wasn't important enough.

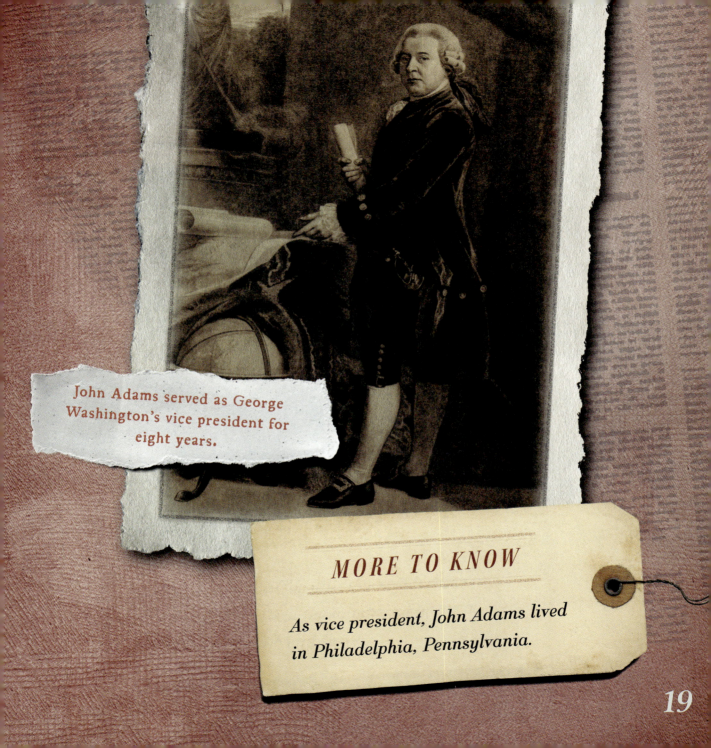

John Adams served as George Washington's vice president for eight years.

MORE TO KNOW

As vice president, John Adams lived in Philadelphia, Pennsylvania.

REMEMBERING PRESIDENT
JOHN ADAMS

Adams ran for president again in 1796. This time, Adams won the election. He was part of the Federalist **political party**. This party believed in a strong central government.

John Adams only served one term as president. In 1800, he lost the election to Thomas Jefferson. He returned to his home in Quincy, Massachusetts, where he spent much of his time writing about politics and his life. On July 4, 1826, John Adams died at 90 years old.

MORE TO KNOW

Following in his father's footsteps, John Adams's son also ran for president. In 1825, John Quincy Adams became the sixth president of the United States.

PRESIDENT ADAMS'S TIMELINE

1755
Adams completes his education at Harvard College.

1758
Adams starts working as a lawyer in Massachusetts.

MARCH 5, 1770
The Boston Massacre takes place.

1774
Adams joins the First Continental Congress.

1783
The Treaty of Paris is signed.

1797
Adams is elected as the second president of the United States.

OCTOBER 30, 1735
John Adams is born in Braintree, Massachusetts.

1756
Adams starts studying law in Massachusetts.

1764
Adams and Abigail Smith are married.

OCTOBER – DECEMBER 1770
Adams defends the British soldiers who were charged for the Boston Massacre.

1776
Adams helps write the Declaration of Independence.

1789
Adams becomes the first vice president of the United States under George Washington.

JULY 4, 1826
John Adams dies at 90 years old.

GLOSSARY

American Revolution: The war in which the colonies won their freedom from England.

client: A person who pays for professional services, or services somebody provides as their job.

committee: A small group that does a certain job.

democracy: The free and equal right of every person to participate in a government.

encourage: To make a person more hopeful, confident, or determined to do something.

essay: A piece of writing.

lawyer: Someone whose job it is to help people with their questions and problems with the law.

negotiate: To come to an agreement.

political party: A group of people with similar beliefs about how government should be run who try to win elections together.

politics: The activities of the government and government officials.

FOR MORE INFORMATION

BOOKS

Elston, Heidi M. D. *John Adams*. Minneapolis, MN: Checkerboard Library, 2021.

Krajnik, Elizabeth. *Team Time Machine Picks a President in the Election of 1800*. New York, NY: Gareth Stevens Publishing, 2021.

WEBSITES

Britannica Kids: John Adams
https://kids.britannica.com/kids/article/John-Adams/345449
Learn more about John Adams's life and presidency.

National Geographic Kids: John Adams
https://kids.nationalgeographic.com/history/article/john-adams
Find out more about John Adams.

Publisher's note to educators and parents: Our editors have carefully reviewed these websites to ensure that they are suitable for students. Many websites change frequently, however, and we cannot guarantee that a site's future contents will continue to meet our high standards of quality and educational value. Be advised that students should be closely supervised whenever they access the internet.

INDEX

Adams, John Quincy, 16, 20

birthday, 4

birthplace, 4

British soldiers, 10, 21

brothers, 5

Continental Congress, 14, 21

Declaration of Independence, 14, 15, 21

farming, 6

father, 6, 7

Great Britain, 12, 16

home, 7, 20

Jefferson, Thomas, 14, 15, 20

letters, 9

parents, 4

Philadelphia, Pennsylvania, 19

school, 6, 7

Smith, Abigail, 8, 9, 21

sons, 16

Treaty of Paris, 16, 17, 21

vice presidency, 18, 19, 21

Washington, George, 13, 18, 19, 21